GOODBYE
2019
HELLO
2020

First published in the United Kingdom in 2019 by
Pavilion
43 Great Ormond Street
London
WC1N 3HZ

ISBN 978-1-911641-61-2

A CIP catalogue record for this book is available from the British
Library.

10 9 8 7 6 5 4 3 2 1

Reproduction by Mission Productions Ltd, Hong Kong
Printed and bound by IMAK Ofset, Turkey

www.pavilionbooks.com

GOODBYE 2019 HELLO 2020

CREATE A LIFE YOU LOVE THIS YEAR

Project Love | PAVILION

Oscar Wilde

TO LIVE IS THE RAREST THING IN THE WORLD.

MOST PEOPLE EXIST, THAT IS ALL.

Goodbye 2019,
Hello 2020

As one year comes to an end and another begins, it's time for you to take a step back. To pause for a moment in the rush of life. And reflect.

Reflect on the year you've just lived. And the year that lies ahead.

To recognize and acknowledge all that you've been through, all that you've done and all that you're grateful for having experienced in the last 12 months: the lessons, the love, the achievements, the people and the moments that marked this year and made it unique.

It's time to let yourself dream, ask yourself what you really want and then, with courage and conviction, commit to making that happen.

So let's do that.

Let's say a proper farewell to 2019 and get ready to make 2020 a year to remember!

How this
journal works

Goodbye 2019, Hello 2020 guides you through a journey that helps you say a proper farewell to 2019, as it comes to an end, and create a vision and a plan for you to thrive and live a life you love in the year to come.

You'll begin by reflecting on all that has happened in your life in 2019 – your happiest moments, your achievements, the challenges you've overcome and the people you're grateful for. Then, through a series of questions and exercises, you'll be encouraged to think about what you need in life to feel happy, fulfilled and full of love. You'll use those ingredients to choose what you'd most like to focus on in 2020 and which dreams you'd like to bring to life.

By the end of the book you will have in your hands a vision for the life you want to live in 2020, the dreams you want realized and a simple plan for how you're going to make it all happen.

Goodbye 2019, Hello 2020 will become your motivational journal for designing a life you love in 2019, with quarterly check-ins to help you keep on track throughout the year.

Remember, there is no right or wrong way to answer any of the questions in the book. Relax, have fun with it and just see what answers emerge on the page.

Don't worry if with some questions you draw a blank – you can always come back to them later or skip them all together. Not every question will be relevant for you this year.

For every question, you'll find you have a few lines to write your answer. If you think that you need more space, there are some extra blank pages at the back of the book.

We have loved seeing what *Goodbye, Hello* has done for people over the past nine years and now we can't wait to see what it will do for you!

Share with us!

There is nothing we love more than seeing photos of you using your *Goodbye, Hello* journal. It is so exciting to see people all over the world dreaming and designing their lives into the pages of this book and sharing their experiences with us.

Share a photo of you doing your *Goodbye, Hello* journal with us:

⊙ @loveprojectlove

#thegoodbyehellojournal

✉ hello@loveprojectlove.com

x Selina & Vicki

Jo Ann Davis

OUR SOULS NEED TIME TO THINK, DREAM AND REFLECT.

Goodbye 2019

A lot can change, a lot can happen in just one year.

Let's see what happened in your life...

What happened in your life in 2019?

So, here we are at the end of another year. The Earth has completed another full circle around the Sun. And in those 12 months your life has been a mixture of happy and sad moments, things to celebrate and challenges to overcome. And throughout it all you have grown and learned in the process.

Now it's time to take a moment, step back and reflect on the year you've just lived.

Over the following pages you'll be answering questions designed to help you recall your biggest moments from 2019: your happiest memories, the problems you've solved and the biggest lessons you've learned.

If at first you find it hard to recall things then take it slowly. Go month by month, perhaps using your calendar to help remind you of what you got up to over the past year.

Remember that there are no right or wrong answers to any of these. You might have just a few lines to write for one question, but with others, you might have so much you want to write you'll need to use the extra pages at the back of the book.

The key is to relax, spend a little time pondering each question and enjoy remembering all the things that happened in 2019...

Maya Angelou

WE DELIGHT IN THE BEAUTY OF THE BUTTERFLY, BUT RARELY ADMIT THE CHANGES IT HAS GONE THROUGH TO ACHIEVE THAT BEAUTY.

What was going on in your life this time last year?

How were you feeling?

As you looked ahead into 2019, what did you want it to be all about for you?

What happened
in 2019?

What were the main events and milestones in your life in 2019?

What did you create, achieve and make happen in 2019 (the big and the small)?

What were your happiest moments?

When did you have the most fun?

When and where did you feel the most at peace?

What has been the most unexpected thing about this year?

What new thing(s) did you discover about yourself?

What time did you love the most?

What are you particularly proud of?

What have been your hardest moments in 2019?

What have been your biggest challenges?

What are the most important lessons you have learned?

Gratitude

Shauna Niequist

WHEN LIFE IS SWEET, SAY THANK YOU AND CELEBRATE. AND WHEN LIFE IS BITTER SAY THANK YOU AND GROW.

The power
of gratitude

Gratitude is the simple but powerful practice of expressing thanks and giving appreciation for what you have in your life, right now.

Research shows that the practice of gratitude improves your health, increases your happiness and productivity and helps you to foster deep and fulfilling relationships.

And it is a key tool when it comes to designing a life you love.

Because whatever you focus your attention on, you get more of. Thinking about what you are grateful for, rather than envying what you are lacking, helps to keep you in a positive mindset; the life you dream of feels perfectly possible. Your actions and choices then align with that dream life, help invite it in and make it happen.

Let's create more of what you want in life by taking some time to reflect on all that you're grateful for having in your life right now...

At the moment, what are you grateful for in your life?

Who are you grateful for?

What about yourself are you grateful for this year?

THERE IS ONE PERSON IN THE WORLD THAT KNOWS BETTER THAN ANYONE HOW TO MAKE YOU HAPPY. THAT PERSON IS YOU.

What do you want to fill your life with?

Now that you've said a proper farewell to 2019, it's time to turn your attention towards 2020. Look at the fresh new canvas ahead of you and choose what you want to fill it with.

In order for you to be able to do that, you first need to be clear on what it is you need in life to feel happy, alive, fulfilled and full of love. This year and beyond.

And that is what this next section is all about.

Over the following pages, you're going to build up a juicy list of all the things that make you happy in life: the things you love to do, the people you love to spend your time with and the places you love to spend your time in.

You're going to look back to some of your happiest times in life and the ingredients that helped to make you so happy then and you're going to allow yourself to imagine what you would love your dream life to look like five years from now.

As in the previous section, there are no right or wrong answers to any of these questions. You might have loads to write for one and just a sentence to write on the next. And don't be surprised if you find yourself repeating some answers – this just helps to highlight what is particularly important to you at the moment.

So relax your mind, let your imagination go and see what emerges on the page in front of you as you start to write...

Hello you

LET YOUR HEART GUIDE YOU. IT WHISPERS, SO LISTEN CLOSELY.

What makes you feel happy, alive and fulfilled in life?

What are the things
you love to do?

What simple pleasures do you enjoy?

What activities make you come alive?

What activities help you to feel calm and relaxed?

What do you love to do on your time off or on weekends?

What do you love to do on holiday?

What are the things that you could spend all day doing and never get tired of?

What activities do you love to do with the people you love?

What activities do you love to do on your own?

Think back to your happiest moments in life – what were you doing that made you so happy?

Where are the places you love to spend time in?

Where do you feel your happiest? (This can be a specific place such as at home, or a more general area – by the sea, for example.)

What places (or kinds of places) do you feel most at peace and relaxed?

Where are the places that you have the most fun?

What are the kinds of places you like to visit on holiday?

What places in the world would you one day love to visit?

Think back to your happiest moments in life – where were you that made you so happy?

Who are the people you love to be with?

Who are the people that make you happy in life?

Who are the people you feel most loved by?

Who are the people that inspire you most in life? (You can include people you know, people you follow online or even fictional or historical characters.)

Who are the people you feel you can be most yourself with? And why?

Who are the people that really see your value?

How do you love to feel?

When you're at your happiest at home, how do you feel?

When you're at your happiest at work, how do you feel?

When you're at your happiest on your own, how do you feel?

When you're at your happiest among people, how do you feel?

What life do you dream of?

Take your
dreams seriously

Our ability to dream and then make those dreams happen is the magic we have as human beings.

It is what gives us the power to be able to bring about change in our own lives and in the world around us.

And it is therefore a key tool when it comes to designing a life you truly love.

So, over the following few pages, you're going to allow yourself to dream. And dream BIG.

Let yourself imagine that anything is possible and see what dreams emerge when you allow yourself to do that...

Anonymous

NEVER LET IT BE SAID THAT TO DREAM IS A WASTE OF ONE'S TIME. FOR DREAMS ARE OUR REALITIES IN WAITING. IN DREAMS, WE PLANT THE SEEDS OF OUR FUTURE.

Your dream life

The key to dreaming and dreaming BIG is to give yourself permission. Permission to imagine that anything is possible and to dream from there.

So let's imagine you have a magic wand that you can use to conjure up whatever you want in your own life: your dream home, dream career, dream relationship – whatever it is you want, you can have it.

Now imagine that you're living that life five years from now.

Take yourself there for a moment and describe what that life is like. And don't hold back. Let yourself dream as wildly as your imagination allows...

Where do you live?

What is your home like?

How do you spend your days?

What do you do on your time off?

What kind of holidays do you go on?

Who are the special people in your life?

What have you achieved over the past five years? (Remember that this is five years into the future.)

Is there anything else you can see in this dream life of yours?

How does it feel to live this life?

What is it that you love the MOST about this life of yours?

Anonymous

GO CONFIDENTLY IN THE DIRECTION OF YOUR DREAMS AND LIVE THE LIFE YOU HAVE IMAGINED.

As you look at your 'dream life', which parts do you want to start introducing the most in 2020?

What practical steps can you take to get started on bringing those dreams to life in 2020?

Hello 2020

William Ernest Henley

I AM THE MASTER OF MY FATE, I AM CAPTAIN OF MY SOUL.

Hello 2020

A fresh new year lies ahead of you. A blank canvas for you to paint with the things you love. A whole new chapter in your life for you to write.

So... what do you want to fill your life with in 2020? What do you want it to be all about?

It's time to choose.

As you look back at your answers in this journal so far, you can see which dreams are calling to you the most, which ingredients will make you most happy this year and what you want to choose as your 2020 focus.

Over the following pages you'll be asked questions designed to help you to get clear on what you want to make your 2020 all about.

You'll start by understanding what you need to feel alive and well in your body on a day-to-day basis. Your wellbeing is vital to your happiness, so living a life you love always begins with self-care. From there you will then choose what it is you want to focus on in 2020.

As with every other section, you will likely find that there are some questions you have clear answers for, while others don't feel so relevant to you this year. Don't worry if you don't have an answer to every question. Just answer the ones that speak to you.

So let's turn the page and start designing your 2020...

Wellbeing – the foundation to your happiness

It's difficult to enjoy your life, no matter how good it is, if you feel tired, stressed or burnt out most of the time. And so making sure you give your mind and body what they need to feel energized, focused and calm on a daily basis is essential to designing a life you love.

So let's see what wellbeing activities and practices you can lay at the foundations of your life in 2020.

What can you do on a daily or weekly basis to help you feel good in your body? *For example, running, dancing, yoga, eight hours of sleep, drinking plenty of water.*

What can you do on a daily or weekly basis to help you remain calm and grounded? *For example, meditation, having a bath in the evening, getting out in nature, journalling and so on.*

How do you relax and unwind at the end of the day or at the weekend (in a way that doesn't involve alcohol, a TV screen or your phone)?

When you're under pressure and spinning a lot of plates, what can you do throughout the day to help keep you calm, relaxed, focused and positive?

When you're worn out and need some serious rest, what helps you to restore your energy and recharge your batteries?

What do you want to make
your 2020 all about?

Which of your dreams do you want to bring to life this year (or start to bring to life)?

What changes (if any) do you want to make in your life in 2020?

What challenges do you want to take on (if any) in 2020?

How do you want to see yourself grow in 2020?

What else do you want to do or make happen in 2020?

What else do you want your life to be full of in 2020?

People, places, activities, holidays, experiences...

Read through your answers on pages 30–46 and copy down the ones you most want to make sure you fill your life with in 2020...

What do you want to
feel in 2020?

Look back at your answers on how you love to feel on pages 38–9 and, below, circle the feelings that call out to you and add any of your own...

Calm, joy, fun, peace, happiness, love, inspiration, connection, focus, playfulness, power, contentment, fulfilment, nourishment, vitality, abundance, freedom, gratitude, ease, serenity, courage, passion, stillness, strength, softness, integrity, lightness, celebration, generosity, balance, kindness, wonder, commitment, optimism, unity, purpose, clarity, compassion...

Now circle one to three feelings that you most want to experience in 2020.

In 2020 I want to feel...

What do you want to make your 2020 all about?

The power of choosing
a focus for your year

OK, now we are getting to the big moment in your *Goodbye, Hello* journey: it's time for you to choose your focus for the year.

What do you want to make 2020 all about? What do you want your focus to be?

Having a focus for your year acts like a guiding star, helping to guide your choices and actions in the direction of your dreams.

It is a way for you to commit seriously; to you, your happiness and your wellbeing. And to creating a life you love.

Over the following pages you'll find guidance on how to choose your focus, but ultimately it is simply about choosing a focus that makes you feel good when you imagine a whole year of making that a priority.

So have a read through the different ways you can choose your focus, look back over the previous pages in this section and choose a focus that really makes you smile.

Tony Robbins

WHERE FOCUS GOES, ENERGY FLOWS.

How to choose
your focus

The most important thing is that you choose a focus that feels good to you. Never choose a focus for your year because you think you should or because you think it sounds good. Choose a focus for your year that gets you feeling excited and looking forward to the year that lies ahead.

Here are a few different ways you can choose your focus for the year:

Option 1: Choose something that you want more of in your life in 2020.

You might be craving more of something in your life like...

Creativity, fun, love, calm, adventure, celebration, nourishment, joy, laughter, peace, clarity, gratitude, self-care, connection, femininity, vitality, self-love, magic.

And so you could make that your focus for 2020 and commit to cultivating and bringing more of that into your life in the year to come.
'2020 is my year of fun.'
'2020 is my year of creativity.'
'2020 is my year of self-care.'

Option 2: Choose an intention for the year.

Maybe as you've been answering your questions in your journal so far you've felt a desire to really set an intention for this year. You might not know how it's going to manifest, but that is part of the magic of it: you set the intention and see how it grows. You just know that this is what you want to make this year all about.

'2020 is my year of stepping into my power.'
'2020 is my year of standing in love.'
'2020 is my year of designing a life I love.'
'2020 is my year of healing.'
'2020 is my year of saying 'yes!''

Option 3: Choose a big change you want to make or a big dream you want to bring to life.

Maybe this is the year where you really feel ready to commit and make that big change happen or bring that big dream to life. And so that is what you want to choose as your 2020 focus to really fire up your commitment and make it your central focus for the year.

'2020 is my year of starting my own business.'
'2020 is my year of finding an exciting new career path.'
'2020 is my year of buying my first home.'
'2020 is my year of creating my home in a new country.'
'2020 is my year of taking a six-month sabbatical.'

That said, even if you do have a big change you want to make or big dream you want to bring to life in 2020, you don't have to choose that as your focus. You might prefer to focus on how you want to approach making that change. For example you might want 2020 to be the year that you really get your career change going, but rather than making 2020 your year of 'career change' you might choose to make it your year of 'self care', to help you focus on looking after your wellbeing while you go through a big life change.

Option 4: Just go with what your gut says.

If you just *know* what you want your focus for 2020 to be, even if it doesn't fit into Options 1 to 3, then go for it. The key with choosing your focus is that it is meaningful and inspiring to *you*.

Now it's time for you to choose a focus for your 2020...

2020
is my year of

....

Why do you want that to be your focus for 2020?

So let's make it happen!

How to design a life
you love in 2020

Designing a life you love doesn't happen by accident. Whatever your dreams, your desires, your visions for this year and the future, it isn't luck that will make them happen. It is you taking action that will ultimately have you creating a life you love.

So now it's time to come up with as many things as you can think of that will help you make 2020 your year of:

....

You can choose big things and small things.

For example, if you chose 2020 to be your year of 'Adventure' then maybe there are a few big adventures you know you want to go on in 2020 or that you already have booked. Write those down. But don't stop there. What other things could you do to bring adventure into your life this year, even in small ways? Really have some fun with this and if you struggle with coming up with ideas, ask a friend to help brainstorm ideas with you.

On the next page, write down at least 10 things you could do this year to bring your dreams and intentions to life. And do come back to this list and add things to it, as and when you think of them.

All the things I could do, big or small, to make 2020 my year of:

COMMITMENT IS THE MAGIC INGREDIENT THAT TRANSFORMS YOUR DREAMS INTO YOUR REALITY.

Choose three things to focus on first...

Now it's time to choose THREE THINGS that you're going to do between now and April that have you committing to your focus for 2020 and creating a life you love.

Why just three things?

Because we have found over the years that three is the magic number when it comes to setting goals and actually making them happen.

It keeps them memorable and manageable and therefore far more likely to succeed.

Now there is one simple rule to choosing your three commitments; they have to feel good to you. You can stretch yourself with a commitment that kind of scares you (big commitments usually do), but only if the fear is matched with excitement. And no choosing a commitment because you think you should. Designing a life you love will never grow out of doing things just because you think you should.

So choose the three practical steps that appeal to you the most at the moment.

And finally, get specific. If one of your commitments, for example, is to learn Spanish then don't just write down 'I'm going to learn Spanish'. Get specific about how, when and where: 'I'm going to find a Spanish teacher to have a lesson with once a week' or 'I'm going to spend two hours every Wednesday studying Spanish via an online course'.

And then open up your calendar and schedule in the first step you're going to take to get that commitment going (for example, 'research Spanish teachers in my area').

What I will do
January – March 2020

The three things I commit to doing between now and 31 March:

1.

2.

3.

Declare it

Now that you have your focus for 2020 and your commitments between now and April set, it is time for the final step: to declare your focus and commitments to the world.

Because it is when you start sharing with others what your game plan for 2020 is that the magic really begins.

Opportunities start to appear, things seem to align themselves, you'll suddenly notice paths towards your dream that you might never have thought of before.

So it is time to declare your 2020 focus to someone in your life. Someone who counts. Someone who loves and supports you and wants to see you live a life you love.

Who will that person be?

....

Let them know what you are committing to doing in 2020 and ask that they hold you to account.

Brené Brown

TALK TO YOURSELF LIKE YOU WOULD TO SOMEONE YOU LOVE.

A message from
you to you

Learning to give yourself the words of encouragement and support you need to help you go forward into the world and create a life you love is every bit as important as creating a plan and action steps that will bring those dreams to life.

However, most of us tend to be our own harshest critics and we are more tuned into the negative, critical side of ourselves that is ready to point out where we're failing and cast doubt over whether we really have what it takes to make our dreams happen. We often only use our loving supportive side on our loved ones. Now it's time to turn that loving attention towards yourself.

Let that side of you write a message of encouragement to you as you step into 2020 ready to make you and your happiness a top priority and ready to create a life you love...

My message from me to me...

And so the journey begins...

Mastin Kipp

WHEN YOU TAKE A STEP TOWARDS YOUR SOUL - THE LIFE YOU'RE MEANT TO BE LIVING TAKES A MASSIVE LEAP TOWARDS YOU.

Designing a life
you love in 2020

Designing a life
you love in 2020

One of the main problems with our traditional New Year's resolutions is that we create a list of the things we'd like to achieve over the course of the year, get excited about it and then by the time we've hit February we've got caught up in the rush of life and our sparkly list of New Year's resolutions has been pretty much forgotten.

According to research only 8% of New Year's resolutions ever happen and 50% fail within the first month.

So with *Goodbye, Hello* we do things differently.

We get you to hold onto just one main focus for the year and then commit to doing just three things every three months that will help you to stick to your focus for 2020 and design a life you love.

At the start of every quarter (that is, the start of April, July and October) we bring you back to your *Goodbye, Hello* journal so that you can check in with yourself, reflect on the previous three months and revisit your three commitments to see how you got on.

You then set three fresh new commitments for the following three months. Commitments that support you in creating a life that you love.

Come and follow us over on Instagram and we'll remind you at the start of each quarter when it's time for your quarterly check-in.

⊙ @loveprojectlove

Living a life you love doesn't happen by accident.

It isn't down to luck.

It's down to you.

Remind yourself of your dreams on a regular basis and keep taking practical steps until you've made those dreams come true.

Quarterly
check-ins

Anonymous

THE FUTURE BELONGS TO THOSE WHO BELIEVE IN THE BEAUTY OF THEIR DREAMS.

April

April Reflections

How are you feeling at the moment?

What happened in your life since January?

What have you done that you're proud of?

What were your happiest moments?

What were your most challenging moments?

What and who are you grateful for at this moment in your life?

April Check-in

Go and take a look at your focus for 2020 and the three things you committed to doing. It's time to review how things have been going:

What have you done from that list of commitments?

What haven't you done from that list of commitments?

If there is anything you didn't do from that list of commitments then what do you think has got in the way of you doing it?

Do you want to carry this commitment through to the next quarter? If you do, then what can you do to make sure you prioritize it between now and 30 June?

What else would you like to do between now and 30 June to help you create a life you love?

Now choose the THREE THINGS you most want to commit to doing over the next three months and write them down on the next page.

What I will do
April – June 2020

The three things I commit to doing between now and 30 June:

1.

2.

3.

W. H. Murray

WHATEVER YOU CAN DO OR DREAM YOU CAN, BEGIN IT. BOLDNESS HAS GENIUS, MAGIC & POWER IN IT.

July

July Reflections

How are you feeling at the moment?

What happened in your life since April?

What have you done that you're proud of?

What were your happiest moments?

What were your most challenging moments?

What and who are you grateful for at this moment in your life?

July Check-in

Go and take a look at your focus for 2020 and the three practical steps you committed to taking between April and now. It's time to review how things have been going:

What have you done from that list of commitments?

What haven't you done from that list of commitments?

If there is anything you didn't do from that list of commitments, then what do you think has got in the way of you doing it?

Do you want to carry this commitment through to the next quarter? If you do, then what can you do to make sure you prioritize it between now and 30 September?

What else would you like to do between now and 30 September to help you create the life you love?

Now choose the THREE THINGS you most want to commit to doing over the next three months and write them down on the next page.

What I will do
July – September 2020

The three things I commit to doing between now and 30 September.

1.

2.

3.

H. Jackson Brown

NEVER GIVE UP ON WHAT YOU REALLY WANT TO DO. THE PERSON WITH BIG DREAMS IS MORE POWERFUL THAN ONE WITH ALL THE FACTS.

October

October Reflections

How are you feeling at the moment?

What happened in your life since July?

What have you done that you're proud of?

What were your happiest moments?

What were your most challenging moments?

What and who are you grateful for at this moment in your life?

October Check-in

Go and take a look at your focus for 2020 and the three practical steps you committed to taking between 1 July and now. It's time to review how things have been going:

What have you done from that list of commitments?

What haven't you done from that list of commitments?

If there is anything you didn't do from that list of commitments, then what do you think has got in the way of you doing it?

Do you want to carry this commitment through to the next quarter? If you do, then what can you do to make sure you prioritize it between now and 31 December?

What else would you like to do between now and 31 December to help you create the life you love?

Now choose the THREE THINGS you most want to commit to doing over the next three months and write them down on the next page.

What I will do
October – December 2020

The three things I commit to doing between now and 31 December:

1.

2.

3.

Patti Smith

WE GO THROUGH LIFE, WE SHED OUR SKINS, WE BECOME OURSELVES.

Notes